Greeting ___

Poems for the Holidays

by Rita A. Simmonds

Cover: ***The Nativity,*** **watercolor by Carrie A. Bucalo**

ACKNOWLEDGMENTS

These poems, some in significantly different versions, have appeared in *MAGNIFICAT* magazine:
"The Gift"
"Living Memory"
"Constant Crèche"
"Word Made Flesh"
"Our Lady of God's Garden"
"Our Lady of Guadalupe"
"At the Manger All Are Fed"
"The Sign of Conversion"
"Bclow thc Star"
"Rembrandt's *Return of the Prodigal Son*"
"This Advent"

"Magi Admitted" was published in *PILGRIM: A Journal of Catholic Experience*

"Joy in July" was published in *tall...ish Pure Slush Vol. 11*

For My Mother
who makes holidays happy and holy

Table of Contents

The Journey
based on "The Nativity" watercolor by Carrie Bucalo

A sky so filled with constellations
at last displays the essential star.
We need decode no more
but simply follow what is most pronounced—
what we cannot help but heed.

We discerned a cross on the mountain top
still a long way off,
and thought that would be our aim
until we caught sight of a warm light
at the foot of the hill
seeming to rise to meet us
as we moved quickly toward

nothing but a family
huddled in a cove—
but we were explorers
and had to know
yet somehow couldn't ask.

The baby slept
the mother smiled
the father watched,
and held his staff.

No one said a word.

From science we learned to observe.
In silence we learned to adore.
We gave our gifts with trembling hands.
Our velvet knelt in straw.
The truth that ruled was plain to see—
we couldn't see it all.

The cross was still a long way off.

The star had led to light.
The journey to the mountain top—
An hour, not this night.

We headed back a different route.
The hour not this night.

The Gift

It's Christmas Eve and we will travel
a long way on a cold night
thinking of the twinkling lights,
the golden bulbs, the heirloom crèche,
the smell of sweets and spice.
A hearty greeting at the door!
The family, friends in velvet clothes
of red and black and gold with bows.
The hugs, the kiss, the Christmas wreath.
In we'll go, and sing and glow
and eat our ham and beef.
We'll join loud fun as one by one
we find our gifts beneath the tree.
We'll toast and tease before the hearth,
kick off our heels, amused and warm—
embraced, enwrapped in Christmas charm.

Now we arrive, and all is hushed.
The place is cold. We see our breath.
The cow and pig have not been killed.
There're lambs and goats alive as well.
The place is full of foreign folk,
battered guests and tattered hosts.
The floor is dirt. There is no tree.
No one has offered food or drink.
We've traveled far but cannot sit.
We see a light and just one Gift.
Is this one Gift for all to share?
This scene is death to Christmas cheer.

I stood and thought of all I'd missed—
until I knelt before the Gift.

Magi Admitted

I'd wondered how it would end,
going all that way at 12am,
driving on and on.
The empty highway
had never been so awakened
from a dream.

What is the world doing now?
Is there another soul around
to share the acuteness
of my need?

At the center of the city,
the avenue bore signs:
Angels dangling from the wire,
wings aflutter without flying.
It's the sentence of the season
for those who seek for things unseen.
You can't buy them in a drug store
like the tinsel red and green,
silver-gray, and yellow-gold,
wrapping railings, swirling poles,
like the chorus girls of ailing step
who every year repeat the show.

With speed I passed beyond the trim,
through traffic lights of red or green.

I ended in a zone unknown,
dodging laughs and screams,
behind a door that locked behind,
I waited for my key.
Parading round the social square
around the nurses' box,
were people of chaotic hair
who swept the floor with socks.

The people of the key approached.
Their coats were dazzling white.
They had no wings, they didn't sing,
but they were most polite.
"Please tell us now
what brought you here?"

What should I say?
What could they hear?

It started with the star, I thought,
the one we've always known about,
the early light we've come to doubt.
I'd seen the slightest evidence
on busy streets or storeroom shelves:
The lights and glitter and tinkling tunes
from wound up tinkering elves.
Or the Santa Clause who rings for alms
deserted by his team.
Such clues as these had led my search,
but now, what did they mean?

But there was no room in the inn
for a question such as this.
Their faces turned my fervor cold,
so I gave them lines that fit:

"I get this way at holidays.
I'm not a danger to myself.
I wish no harm to anyone.
I'm hoping to get well.
I don't expect to be here long.
You'll need my bed.
I'll need your pills.
Just send the bill and I'll be gone."
(I'm sure they knew by heart the song!)

But they marked it down and turned to leave.
"One more question, if you please—
You have the key to free the door,
but do you know where God is born?"

They marked it down and walked away.
I'd find the Babe a different way.

That same night I was stirred from sleep,
by a fellow-traveler, just brought in.
She told me it was snowing out.
I asked her, was it beautiful?
She said she didn't know.
Her face was pale and worn with tears.
She said she'd journeyed twenty years.
"What brought you here?"
She wouldn't say.
Maybe she didn't know.
Her eyes were beginning to show
nothing,
to receive
nothing,
to almost completely close.

"Wise woman! Do you know," I cried,
"the manger where the Baby lies?"

"I've never found Him,
but one thing's sure,
I've lost myself, for what it's worth."

My heart was broken by her words.
"Let's search this scene for signs of birth!"

In haste we met a restless soul
his face reflecting white and red
gazing at the neon sign
above the door we'd all come in.

"I see you always move," I said.

“I wander halls that know no end.”
He pointed to the exit light,
“But still the star of Bethlehem.”

Living Memory

Land, lead my feet
along the path of memory,
and as I walk in the light
of the star
let me gather lambs,
little lambs,
lost sheep,
even innkeepers
overwhelmed
who crack their doors
and peep.

The land unfolds an Infant King.
I saw Him crowned
along the way.
I saw His mother weep.
But now He sleeps
and she receives
all who've lost
and found their way,
and place their journey
at His feet,
hallowed in the hay.

Constant Crèche

We see the star—
white light on pitch,
above the lantern
Joseph's hand
holds in suspense
above the crib
that fills his eyes
with pools of promise,
brimming now and long ago—
Can this be so?
Virgin Bride and Infant Christ
as much his own
as those who enter
in mingling droves
of frankincense and cattle breath,
manured mud and myrrh;
the marveling shepherds,
their jostling herds,
encumbered camels
dismounting kings—
their silken knees
brought down
to earth.

And the Mother too
so lowly bowed
who's never raised her voice
or brow,
but beholds anew
her infant Son,
the timely cave,
the tattered clothes,
the scattered hay,
the offered gold:

The scene she loves

she ponders best—
A constant crèche,
her soul.

Word Made Flesh

A split second
an instant
the flash of an angel's wing—
God uncloaked
and carried
to a tiny place
the most miniscule,
far away
within
invisible,
the most invisibly visible place
the space inside
the Virgin betrothed,
the space of eternal growth.
The heard Word
allowed
to be brought forth
from there
the place of the pact
between Heaven and humankind.
The whole world changed
in an instant
imperceptibly
radically
different
and from that moment on
Eternity came
and has forever stayed
maternally entwined
in time.

Our Lady of God's Garden

I walked with my mother in the garden.
I never lost her hand,
not out of fear
but love
that is need to adhere.
I grew with my mother
like a garden—
turned rich earth,
flourished like fern.
Delight brushed passed.
Only once and enough
I loosed my fleshy grasp
to heed a branching tongue
twining up a tree.
The creature leaned in fast
and breathed on me.
"Take the choicest drupe and eat!"
I snapped the stem and seized the fruit.
It splattered red and stained my palm
but gave no food.
My mother gasped and held her heart.
The creature fell around her feet.
She cracked its neck between her toes.
(Without that slip, my mother's might and sway
I'd never know.)
She cloaked me like the earth
swaddling a seed.
I'll never lose her hand—
Yes, out of fear
and a greater love,
that is greater need
to adhere.

Our Lady of Guadalupe

Mary, the Mexican Lady,
is brown and beautiful,
her cerulean mantle
spotted with stars.

Who could wrap a woman in sky,
as she labors for mankind,
but the One whom she would bear and wrap—
A Gift for all creation's lap?

At the Manger All Are Fed
Love is an exchange of gifts. ~St. Ignatius of Loyola

Mary feeds the flesh of God
with the goodness He has given her.
Israel's King
ingests
the pure, warm milk
of Providence.
The pulse of memory beats
beneath her royal robe,
for there is her treasure
to be pondered
pierced and offered
over and over
in time
and time again.

Body of Christ
built at the Virgin's breast,
do we drink with delight
or forgetfulness?

Gifts at Dawn

In one instant, Eternity was born,
and now there's Christmas Eve.
The angels' singing sweeps the halls
and stirs our spangled sleep.

The still dark day entreats one star
to stay until all come.
The walk, the beasts, the shepherds' dreams
remind us of our own.

We race to find beneath the pine
great treasures from beyond.
Our thrill stops short.
No presents brought!

Our mother's voice stays calm,

"The babe still sleeps,
Now silence keep.
The gifts appear at dawn."

The Sign of Conversion

Bethlehem Star
light years in wait,
releases good news
with celestial gait:
The Word that stirred Heaven
before time began,
is lauded by angels:
the Heart of God's plan.
The power of paradise,
traveling time,
alights on a stable
in silence sublime
that wise men may seek
ageless knowledge foreknown:
The star is the sign,
New Being
the goal.

Below the Star

Wouldn't it be strange
if we all expected nothing—
no change?
Would we wake and stretch
and pray for happiness,
if we expected nothing
from the day?

And yet we doubt
there ever was a birth
that summoned souls
to unfamiliar earth
to trust a guide
no human hand could trace—
the star that shone
infinity in space.

What life will seize
its journey cold and far
without the Light
that shines below the star?

Rembrandt's *Return of the Prodigal Son*

Come and enter this scene,
my friend,
whose light and dark speak Bethlehem.
The single shepherd looks a pauper
donned in rags that reek of fodder.
His knees thus mounted in the earth,
he shrouds his face of noble birth
within the scarlet cloak of one
who cannot help but call him "Son!"

The father's face glows light new-born.
His hands re-hold life once foresworn:
His son of wanton ways untold
whose steps of excess bent him home.

This sudden gift befits a king.
A son is found!
The angels sing!

Simple

The Kingdom of God
is the place so everyday
few are aware
they're even there.

Can you worship
an infant king?
You must ask yourself,
How low can your
homage go?
You will never see
with the eyes that read to analyze
what's between the lines.
You must be surprised
by strange and brilliant change.
You must believe
what you were taught as a child
that you forgot.
You must believe
what you trusted was true.
You must believe
what deep down
you really want to bow before again
because life is so
simple then.

The Thirteenth Day of Christmas

The Christmas tree lights in the corner of the room
still warm the chambers in my heart.
It's past the season to be jolly
and my life lingers on the edge of that beginning.
When the night is still
and a row of little lights smiles on a bough,
He comes brand new
in the afterglow
of holiday cheer
right now
right here.

An Artificial Tree Grows in Brooklyn

Jesus sleeps
below the bough,
an angel dangles
near the cow.

January's come and gone.
My artificial tree
lives on.

Her lights blink red and green,
then white.
She hasn't slept a wink all night.

Her ornaments,
my children's craft—
I read their names
on Santa's hat
or see their faces
framed in "O";
between the "J" and "Y"
they glow.

My husband too,
festooned each day.
The snowman's stomach
bears his name.

We missed the mistletoe
this year.
His life progressed
to Easter cheer.

Joy in July

Red bird
bright
in dark green—
a mid-year reminder
of Christmas Eve.
The bird carols
volumes
from summer leaves—
Sing to me
sing to me
with your whole feathered frame—
the tallest tweet
to the smallest cave.

Summer Pine

Three pinecones gather like a wooden star
atop this summer Christmas tree.

Why do you stand thirsty
so near the rippling tinsel of lake?

Is your time of ornamentation so far away?

You are like a mother who refuses to eat
until her son has returned from the street.

How I hate to see forever green
baked brown and brittle to scentless things.

Why let yourself sag and decay?
Save yourself, I beg!

Is it the breeze that turns you from my plea?
Or do you sigh and turn away?

Oh summer pine, don't change my mind!
Ever's always green.

Evergreen

How straight you stand
with many hands,
clothed in ever-green.
Your limbs have not known nakedness.
The fall has let you be.

Tree Top

Oh Fragility!
You're the top of the tree!
How everything points to you.

Though nimble birds
can bend your nerves,
your greatness is your view.

Ice on Trees

Oh beauty of winter trees!
Your tears that have frozen,
you wear on your sleeves.

Oh tree of crystal trim!
How the wink of the sun
still can dazzle your limbs!

Oh marvel
not to
keep,
the very one who charms you,
makes you
weep.

More About Trees

I

Nature,
so perfect
in your imperfection!
I saw the hand
of your winter tree
extended arthritic
in hopes of having
at least one
star—
so far away
yet hope holds out
until
what's crystal-clear
sheds a
diamond
doubt.

II

Tree,
do you reach for me?
How I love
to look on you,
for you are reaching
while I stay still.
You are my heart
that lives your pose—
hands to the sky
your roots are still.
Desire in winter
wears no clothes.

III
Trees,
if I had your tenacity—
asking all day,
all night,
more in winter.
You spread like webs
extended to the sky...

My dream
is to have
one branch of you
within my heart—
pointed, antlered
penetrating,
making me cry
what's truly aching.

IV
Morning tree
sun touches twigs
in copper mist.
Your limbs awake
to be kissed and kissed.

Heavy Adornment

These trees are heavy with frozen rain,
as if cold tears had stopped their flow
to dress poor limbs in shimmering spears
that make and break boughs beautiful.

Sovereign Tree

A leafless tree
a heightened heart
with branches stretched,
synaptic, sparked.
A pulsing tree
a beating bark
scares me closer
stands up sharp.
A valiant tree
a torch
a king
a dynasty
with roots and rings.
A sovereign tree
from ruptured seed,
a memory
of many leaves.
A living tree
with silent reach
a certain stance
that speaks "just be."

Snow Made Man

I

Your man
stood
plump and pyramid,

built with the electricity of enthusiasm
or Heaven's first
descending winter manna
spread to comfort not to eat but yes partake
in order to con-
struct what may
be construed as
somehow man.

II

Every
flake
we take
collect, reshape
compressing crystals each
distinct
into three spheres of unequal

weight.

What's
stacked and packed is
jabbed and poked with
sticks and stones
and vegetables
to make some likeness to ourselves.

II

Now mark
this

down—
this early flurry,

for the flakes that
fell fell twice.

First on the trees and cars and hills -
a cloak of white that softened chills.

Then as a man
blown

down
by wind
assisted by his rounded base
that rolled him like a tire,
and snapped the twig that tried to break his
fall
as man to earth.

IV

Two days it's been and
still he lies still
intact
wide   open   eyes.
Some snow escapes his central sphere.
One scrawny twig
points to the sky.
His mouth, it frowns a row
of stones.
His carrot nose can't know the scent.
One cannot help but feel sad—

What's only snow
still looks
a man.

Snowflake

Don't make me love you, melting star,
if this one moment's all you are.

A falling flake of feathered glass,
a diamond sculpture dimming fast,
a crystal spark, a polar tear,
a downy dancer swirling spears.
A silver rose, a cloud's regret
that springs a piercing pirouette.
A fleeing hex in artic lace,
a benediction fading grace.

You make me love you, melting star,
and so you are more than you are.

Fast and Lasting Food

Toward the fat smell of fast food
we moved like a herd
coming in from the cold and congealing rain
dragging humanity
hungry for French fries and friendship
waiting in long lines to gain
some comfort covered with ketchup.
We packed our parka-ed selves into a booth
flattened the paper which wrapped our food
and retold our lives between mouthfuls
growing more alive with surprise
having broken every commandment
how we survived.
We were delivered from evil
and in the breaking of the bun
recognized a hallowed childhood
and a Father who is good
to everyone.

Thanksgiving Fast

Thanksgiving was more than a gathering;
it was a collection of characters
captivated by the cornucopic explosion on
our ancient oak table
almost as big as the room it was in.
Everyone was invited:
Joe the farmer
who never bathed in winter,
Aunt Regina
who sat next to him and wheezed,
and my grandmother
who had slowly been losing
her manners and wits.
"The turkey's dry,"
she would say
right after grace.
My father kept us in line with his eyebrows.
My mother would sigh
and continue to serve.
"She always did
make the turkey dry."
We all wanted to laugh.
"But you can't tell her that."
My father looked down
on his vibrating chest
for the moment
had forced him to fast.

This Advent...

prepare a Christmas list.
Don't tell lies
about what you want.
Go outside
and ax the dying tree,
watch it crash in the snow
leaving behind brown and green needles both.
Clear the cupboard
of expired soups and noodles
old antibiotics
stiff marshmallows never melted,
and give away
the fresh box of cereal
the olives and canned tomatoes
flour, salt and sugar.
Don't stuff a turkey
that's already stuffed.
Make room in the refrigerator
for fresh fruit.
Clear your closets.
Give away blankets and boots
jackets and gloves
that no one has worn.
Confess the cobwebs
and skeletons
past celebrations
have kept and ignored.

Standing Invitation

I invite you to enter in.
No need to knock,
but know this:
I expected you long before
this house had a door.
It was built with you in mind,
so step inside;
it's clear
how simple
how neat
it all appears.

This house has many rooms.
Some modern.
Some austere.
Some for children, grown and small.
The couch that doesn't match,
I hesitate to trash.
Let's keep it in the hall
with all your outerwear.

Make yourself uncomfortable.
A wobbly wooden chair
is the perfect place to wonder:
what's the point of being here?

The ceiling is so high.
A living room divine.
You've come to trim the tree?
Don't set the star inside.

What is there to break
but bread?
There's so much crust to crack.
Let's hate to be spoon-fed
but feast beyond our grasp.

You want to leave so fast?
Red wine?
Word Find?
Cartoon?
It's suddenly embarrassing;
I haven't told the truth.

Though I love to entertain
I'm not confident at all.
It took me days and days
to hang a picture on the wall.

My closet's full of games,
but I can't insist we play;
some pieces have gone missing:
dice were rolled and rolled away.

Yet there's boxes full of photographs,
baby toys and books.
Memories in disarray
are less than understood.

In the attic there's a ghost
or a bird that's sound asleep.
Go close or else concede
that it's nothing but a sheet.

I could create nonsensical
and build a house of fun.
Or apologize profusely
for the floors that need redone.
But I'd rather let you wander
in the space that's yours to roam.
If I try too hard to keep you
you will never be at home.

The tour is incomplete

but it's past the time to go.
Don't leave without a sweet!
Keep your pockets full of bread crumbs
for the road.

Greeting the Seasons

Autumn leaves
and long shirt sleeves
and breath that's white
in early night.
Too soon the snow
will come
then go.
And when the earth
seems hard and dead
a sleepy daisy lifts its head.
Before it has
a second yawn,
a restless boy
will mow the lawn.
He doesn't think
but yet he knows
how summer speeds
to hardball throws
that fly through heat
that's chased away
by air that holds
a shorter day.
The boys at bat,
in caps and cleats,
will turn the page
to turning leaves.
On covered trails
they tread to school,
in clothes so stiff
they break the rule.
Though fallen colors
all must die
their smoked remains
ascend the sky.
Before filled lungs
can cough

"good-bye"
or startled thoughts
can form
a "Why?"
Come Holidays
on brassy bells
to horses' rush
that can't be held.
They slip on ice;
they spin away.
The slowest melt
can't help them stay.
The snow gives air
its fairest flake;
what's indistinct
is lost in lake.
But spring unfolds
a luscious scene
a quick "hello"
while it's still green
for all that sliding
into home
brings browner fields
and broken bones.
Yet even boys that limp
will run
and fling their mitts
to hit the sun
as if to set
tall trees ablaze
in orange and golden
autumn glaze.
When vibrant leaves
descend
they cry
and glide to earth
on breezy sigh,
so different from

the brisk “hello”
of wind that slaps around
the snow.

Go nature, rhyme and round the "why?"
Just give us time to say "good-bye."

Made in the USA
Coppell, TX
27 November 2020

42237968R00028